WRITTEN AND ILLUSTRATED BY

Katie Swanson

Dear Sawyer

THE ADVENTURES OF JOVIE AND PAISLEY IN ENGLAND, IRELAND, AND SCOTLAND

DEDICATED TO
MY FUR BABIES, JOVIE AND PAISLEY
AND MY SON, SAWYER JAMES

Enchanted Bonding
BOOKS

EnchantedBondingBooks.com

Sawyer Swanson
140 1st st.
Philadelphia, PA
19092

Sawyer Swanson
140 1st st.
Philadelphia, PA
19092

TAKE GOOD CARE OF MOM AND DAD FOR US.
WE WILL MISS YOU, SAWYER!

zzZ

Dear Sawyer,
Riding on an airplane was so much fun! They gave us delicious snacks and I watched a movie! But I was bummed that the flight attendant wouldn't let me put my head out the window.
♡Paisley

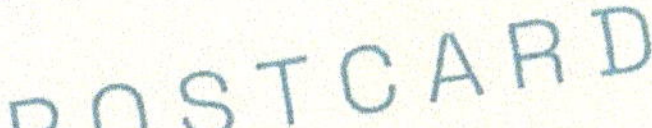

Sawyer Swanson
140 1st st.
Philadelphia, PA
19092

Dear Sawyer,
On the airplane, I took a nice long nap. I'm so thankful that Paisley wasn't allowed to open the window. The wind would have messed up my hair!

♡ Jovie

Sawyer Swanson
140 1st st.
Philadelphia, PA
19092

POSTCARD

Dear Sawyer,
We made it to our first stop
in London, England. Most people
use the underground subway
to get around the city. They
call it "the Tube". We almost
missed our ride though because
Jovie had to give everyone in
the underground station hugs.
♡ Paisley

I made a lot of new friends!

♡ Jovie

POST OFFICE

Sawyer Swanson
140 1st st.
Philadelphia, PA
19092

UNDERGROUND
YOU'RE SO CUTE!
YOU'RE MY NEW BEST FRIEND!
COME ON, JOVIE!

POSTCARD
Dear Sawyer,
Today we visited Warwick Castle and I got to practice my archery skills. I get better the more that I practice!
♡Paisley
POST OFFICE
Sawyer Swanson
140 1st st.
Philadelphia, PA
19092

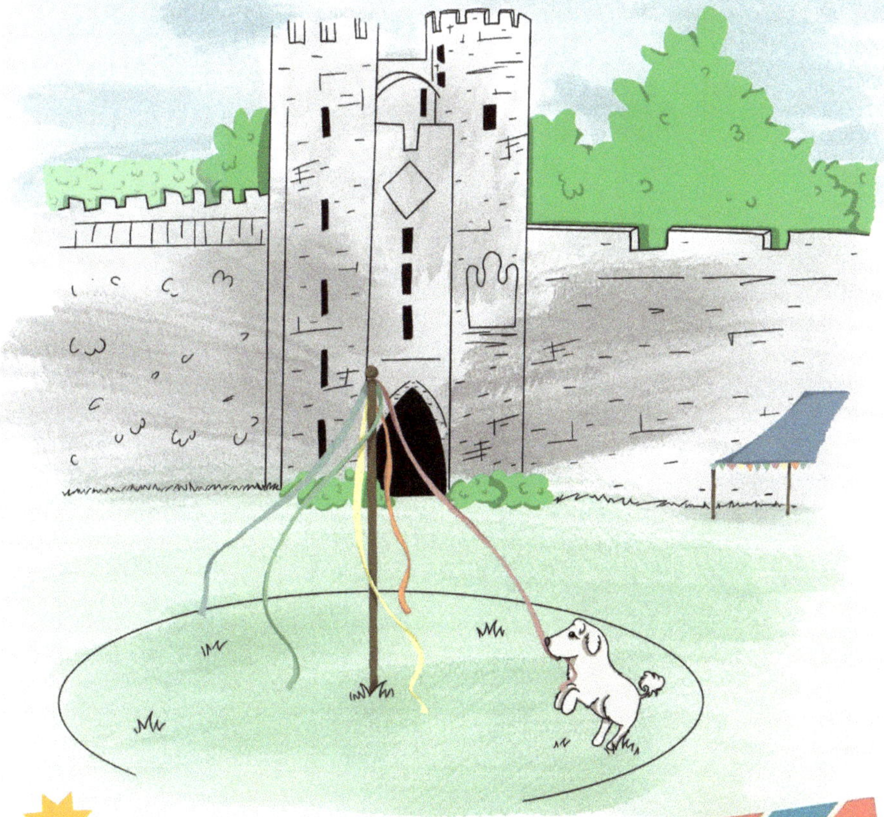

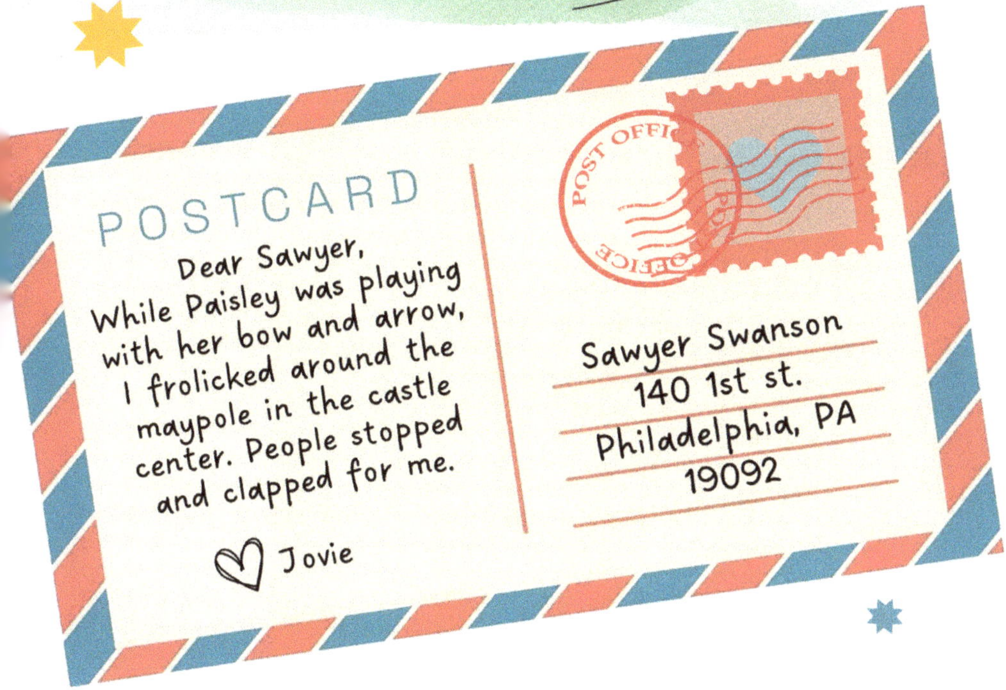

POSTCARD

Dear Sawyer,
While Paisley was playing
with her bow and arrow,
I frolicked around the
maypole in the castle
center. People stopped
and clapped for me.

♡ Jovie

Sawyer Swanson
140 1st st.
Philadelphia, PA
19092

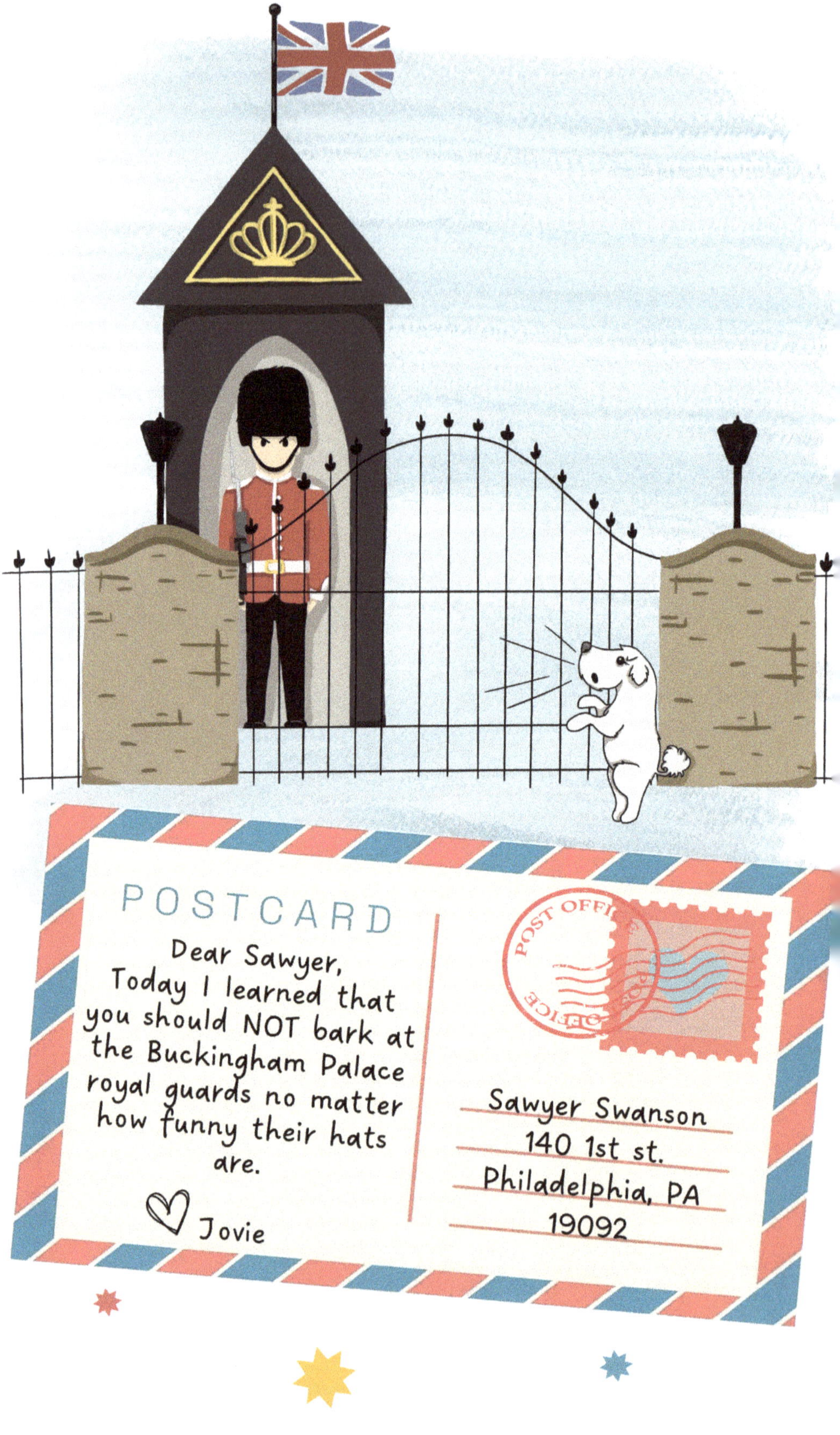

POSTCARD
Dear Sawyer,
Today I learned that you should NOT bark at the Buckingham Palace royal guards no matter how funny their hats are.
Jovie
Sawyer Swanson
140 1st st.
Philadelphia, PA
19092

POSTCARD

Dear Sawyer,
Today I learned that there are a lot of yummy smells inside of those red phone booths. I spent 3 hours investigating with my powerful nose.

♡Paisley

Sawyer Swanson
140 1st st.
Philadelphia, PA
19092

POSTCARD

Dear Sawyer,
We visited a very old town in
England called Stratford-Upon-
Avon. It's where the famous writer
Shakespeare was born. There were
lots of museums and shops to visit.
I smelt something delicious coming
from down the street and
discovered that someone had just
left their fish and chips sitting on
a table! I took the opportunity to
eat a yummy lunch.
♡Jovie

Sawyer Swanson
140 1st st.
Philadelphia, PA
19092

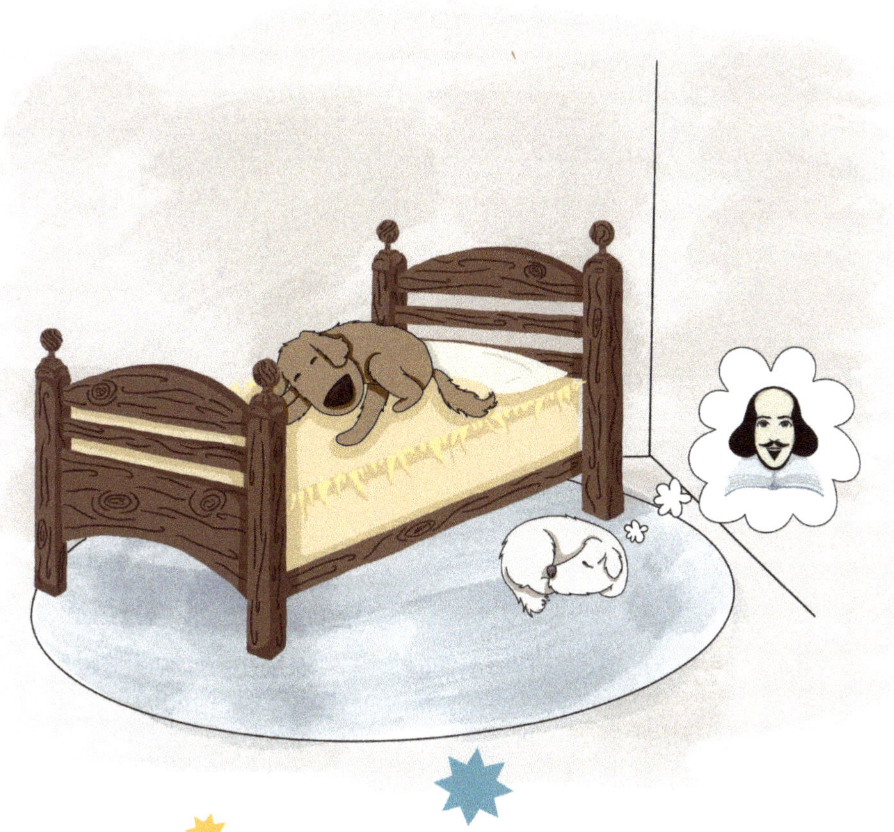

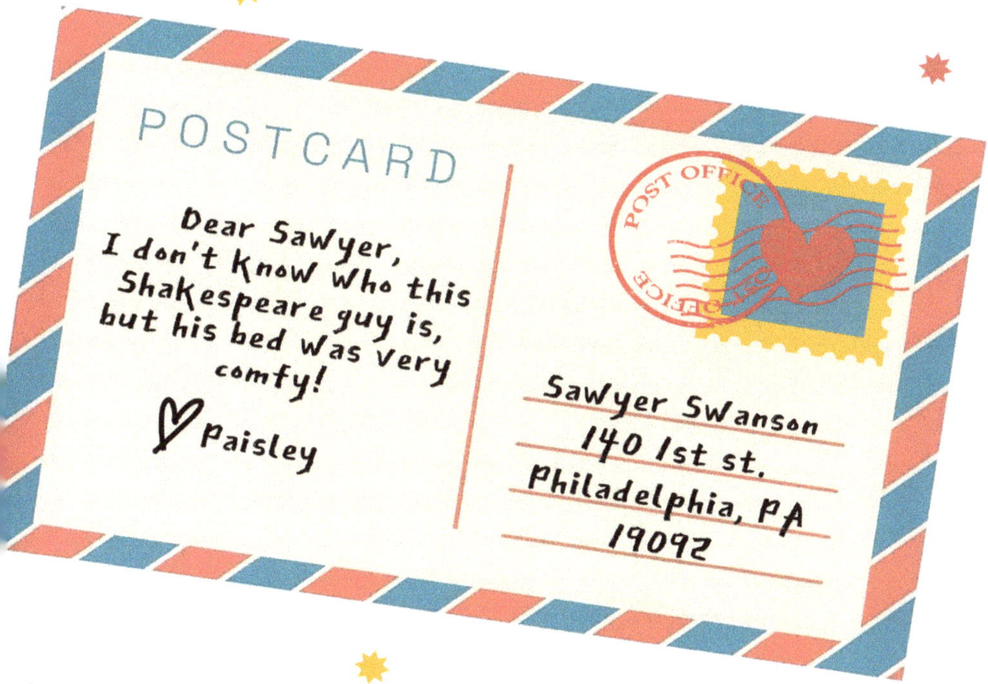

POSTCARD

Dear Sawyer,
I don't know who this
Shakespeare guy is,
but his bed was very
comfy!

♡ Paisley

Sawyer Swanson
140 1st st.
Philadelphia, PA
19092

I'M GOING TO GET YOU!
CATCH ME IF YOU CAN!

POSTCARD

Dear Sawyer,
There is this place in Ireland called Bunratty. The village on the grounds shows how people lived long ago. There is a big castle with swirly stairs and a grand banquet hall where the people who lived there would have feasts.

♡ Jovie

POST OFFICE

Sawyer Swanson
140 1st st.
Philadelphia, PA
19092

POSTCARD

Dear Sawyer,
On the grounds of
Bunratty Castle, I got
to see lots of animals
like goats, donkeys,
and ducks!
♡ Paisley

Sawyer Swanson
140 1st st.
Philadelphia, PA
19092

POST OFFICE

WANT TO BE FRIENDS?
I'M AN IRISH DUCK!

POSTCARD

Dear Sawyer,
One of my favorite parts of
Ireland is a beautiful place
called the Cliffs of Moher.
This is where the green land
meets the blue sea. Jovie and
I spent the day sunbathing
and smelling the ocean air.
♡Paisley
I enjoyed feeling the sunshine
on my belly.
♡Jovie

POST OFFICE
POST OFFICE

Sawyer Swanson
140 1st st.
Philadelphia, PA
19092

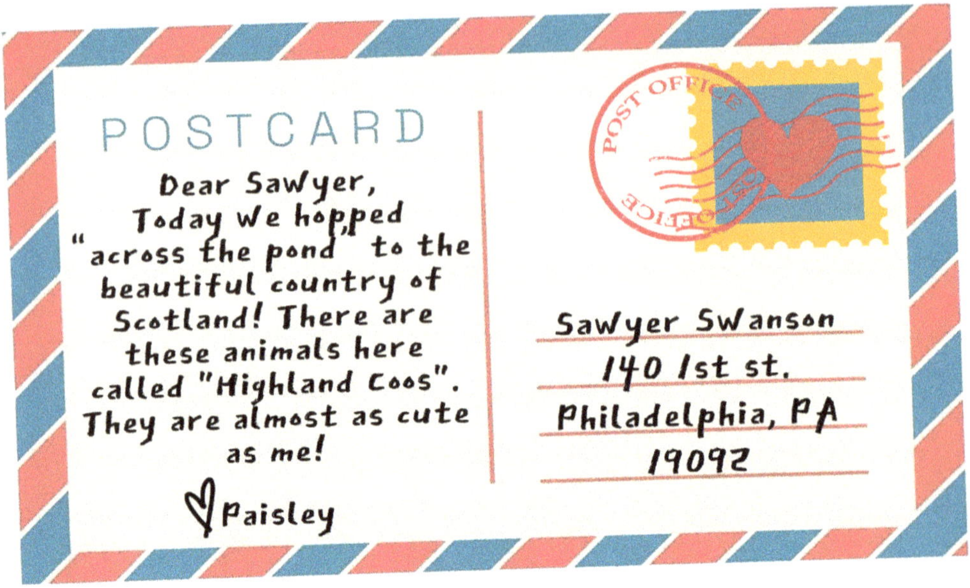

POSTCARD

Dear Sawyer,
Today we hopped "across the pond" to the beautiful country of Scotland! There are these animals here called "Highland Coos". They are almost as cute as me!

♡ Paisley

Sawyer Swanson
140 1st st.
Philadelphia, PA
19092

MY MAMA LOVES YOUR MUSIC.

POSTCARD

Dear Sawyer,
I love Scotland! They play
this special instrument
that has pipes attached to
a large bag. They are called
the bagpipes. They are very
loud.

♡ Jovie

POST OFFICE
POST OFFICE

Sawyer Swanson
140 1st st.
Philadelphia, PA
19092

POST OFFICE
POST OFFICE

POSTCARD
Dear Sawyer,
Scotland has so many
beautiful villages and
grand castles. I could
see US living in a
castle. Couldn't you?
♡Jovie
Sawyer Swanson
140 1st st.
Philadelphia, PA
19092

BOW DOWN, SUBJECTS!

POSTCARD

Dear Sawyer,
Today we went to an event called the highland games. They were throwing very big sticks to win a prize. Apparently they aren't for fetching, though.

♡ Paisley

Sawyer Swanson
140 1st st.
Philadelphia, PA
19092

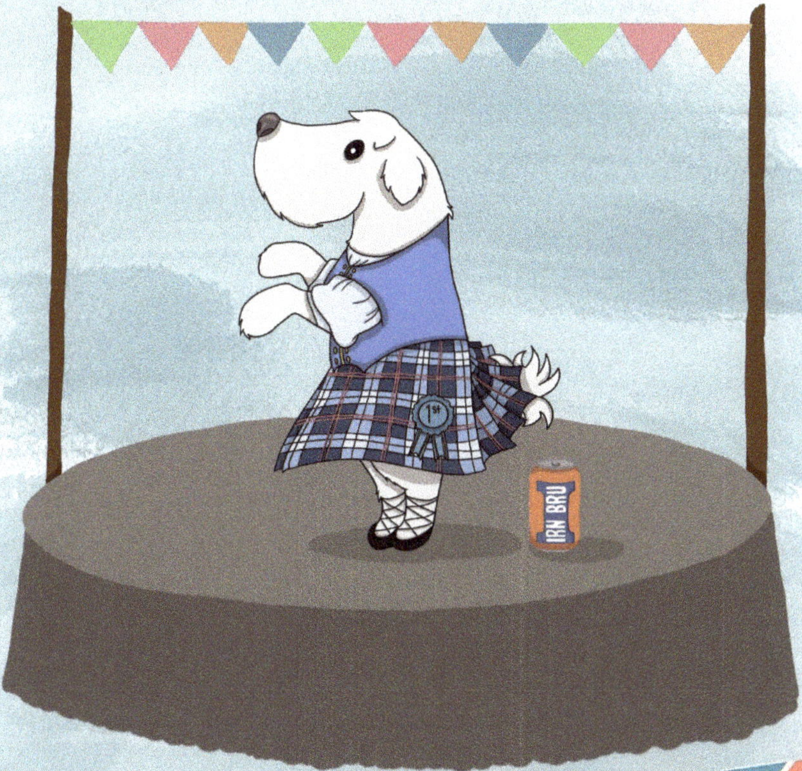

POSTCARD

Dear Sawyer,
I tried this orange drink called Irn Bru. It was tasty, but I wish that it came in peanut butter flavor. Then I tried my paw at highland dancing. I won 1st place!

♡ Jovie

Sawyer Swanson
140 1st st.
Philadelphia, PA
19092

Dear Sawyer,
We took a tour in Edinburgh, Scotland today. We got to visit the castle that sits on top of an extinct volcano. At the very top, there are these things called cannons that fire giant tennis balls!
♡ Paisley

Sawyer Swanson
140 1st st.
Philadelphia, PA
19092

POSTCARD

Dear Sawyer,
We tried a new food called Haggis which is made from the organs of a sheep. It was even tastier than the chicken that dad gives us!

♡ Jovie

Sawyer Swanson
140 1st st.
Philadelphia, PA
19092

POSTCARD

Dear Sawyer,
In the Grass Market village in
Edinburgh, there is a famous
gelato shop called Mary's Milk
Bar. We were in luck, because
they had peanut butter
flavored gelato today! We
shared a treat while enjoying
the view of the Edinburgh
Castle. Paisley tried to hog
the cone though.
♡ Jovie

POST OFFICE

Sawyer Swanson
140 1st st.
Philadelphia, PA
19092

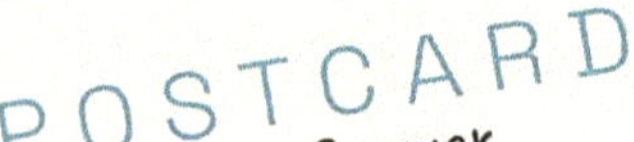

MARY'S MILK BAR
•19•
MARY'S
MILK
BAR

POSTCARD
Dear Sawyer,
Did you know that
Scotland is home to
the fairies? If you
are really lucky, you
can see them dancing
in the lush forests.
♡ Paisley
POST OFFICE
POST OFFICE
Sawyer Swanson
140 1st st.
Philadelphia, PA
19092

POSTCARD

p.s.,
If you leave coins inside of the trees, the
fairies will grant you good health!

SO BEAUTIFUL

POSTCARD

Dear Sawyer,
On the Isle of Skye, we saw
seals sunbathing on the
docks. Then, we went to a
little town called Portree.
Apparently, people live in
very colorful houses here,
but they all looked gray to
me.
♡ Jovie

Sawyer Swanson
140 1st st.
Philadelphia, PA
19092

POSTCARD

Dear Sawyer,
Last night, we slept in a castle! I felt like the true princess that I am.

♡ Jovie

The castle that we spent the night in is called Dalhousie Castle and they had the BEST grass for zoomies!

♡ Paisley

Sawyer Swanson
140 1st st.
Philadelphia, PA
19092

POSTCARD

Dear Sawyer,
Today we visited a lake in
Scotland called Loch Ness.
People in Scotland call "lakes"
"lochs". There is a creature
that lives in Loch Ness named
Nessie. She was a bit shy at
first but we became fast
friends!
♡ Paisley

Nessie scared me so I stayed in
the car.
♡ Jovie

POST OFFICE
POST OFFICE

Sawyer Swanson
140 1st st.
Philadelphia, PA
19092

POSTCARD

Dear Sawyer,
Our trip has come to an end. Although we loved exploring the United Kingdom and Ireland, We missed you so much. We can't wait to snuggle with you!

♥ Paisley

Sawyer Swanson
140 1st st.
Philadelphia, PA
19092

I BROUGHT YOU A SOUVENIR!
I'M SO EXCITED TO SEE YOU, I CAN HARDLY CONTAIN MYSELF!

POSTCARD
Dear Sawyer,
The NEXT time we go on an adventure, YOU are coming with us!
Jovie & Paisley

POST OFFICE
Sawyer Swanson
140 1st st.
Philadelphia, PA
19092

The End

Dear Sawyer

**THE ADVENTURES OF JOVIE AND PAISLEY
IN ENGLAND, IRELAND, AND SCOTLAND**

WRITTEN AND ILLUSTRATED BY

Katie Swanson

2023

About the Author

My name is Katie. I live in the beautiful state of Indiana in the USA. I am a dog mom of a 6-year-old Maltese/Shih-tzu named Jovie and a 2-year-old Miniature Goldendoodle named Paisley (whom the book is inspired by). I am also the mama of a sweet baby boy in Heaven. While I was pregnant with my son, Sawyer, I wrote this book for him. I was so excited for my fur babies to become big sisters and wanted a book that would capture their personalities that I could read to Sawyer. While in my belly, my husband and I read this book to him every night. He'd dance and wiggle around! Unfortunately, Sawyer passed away at 17 hours old in the NICU. We did, however, have a chance to read him this book before he passed away in my arms on August 11, 2023.

After we were married, my husband, Ryan, and I went to the United Kingdom on our honeymoon. We absolutely fell in love with the culture, architecture, and people there. All of the places that Jovie and Paisley go in the book are real places that we visited while on our honeymoon.

Thank you from the bottom of my heart for purchasing and reading this book. My son will never get to read it again, but it fills my heart with love to know that someone out there is getting enjoyment out of this story that I wrote with love for him.

Lots of love,
Katie Swanson

Drinking Irn Bru at the
Highland Games

Me in front of the
Edinburgh Castle

On the grounds of Bunratty
in Ireland